OPTIONS TRADING FOR BEGINNERS

Fundamentals of Options Trading

The How-to Guide to Supplementing your Income with Options Trading

ETHAN BOSON

© Copyright 2020 by Ethan Boson. All right reserved.

The work contained herein has been produced with the intent to provide relevant knowledge and information on the topic on the topic described in the title for entertainment purposes only. While the author has gone to every extent to furnish up to date and true information, no claims can be made as to its accuracy or validity as the author has made no claims to be an expert on this topic. Notwithstanding, the reader is asked to do their own research and consult any subject matter experts they deem necessary to ensure the quality and accuracy of the material presented herein.

This statement is legally binding as deemed by the Committee of Publishers Association and the American Bar Association for the territory of the United States. Other jurisdictions may apply their own legal statutes. Any reproduction, transmission or copying of this material contained in this work without the express written consent of the copyright holder shall be deemed as a copyright violation as per the current legislation in force on the date of publishing and subsequent time thereafter. All additional works derived from this material may be claimed by the holder of this copyright.

The data, depictions, events, descriptions and all other information forthwith are considered to be true, fair and accurate unless the work is expressly described as a work of fiction. Regardless of the nature of this work, the Publisher is exempt from any responsibility of actions taken by the reader in conjunction with this work. The Publisher acknowledges that the reader acts of their own accord and releases the author and Publisher of any responsibility for the observance of tips, advice, counsel, strategies and techniques that may be offered in this volume.

Table of Contents

Introduction 1

Chapter 1: Welcome to Trading Options 4

    How Options Work 5

    Types of Options 10

    Call Option 10

    Put Option 11

    Terms and Conditions 13

Chapter 2: How to Profit from Trading Options.15

    Buy Low, Sell High 18

    Using Options for Speculative Purposes 20

    Writing Contracts 23

Chapter 3: How to Trade Call and Put Options..26

    Buying an Options Contract 27

    Selling an Options Contract 30

    Using Options to Invest with Little Money 33

Chapter 4: Making Money in a Bull or Bear Market 37

    Defining a Bull Market 38

    Defining a Bear Market 40

    How to Make Money During a Bull Market 43

Making Money in a Bear Market............................ 45

Chapter 5: How to Manage Risk in Options Trading 48

Advantage #1: Locking in Prices 50

Advantage #2: Cash Is King 51

Advantage #3: Ensuring Profits 52

Advantage #4: Options Buy You Time 54

Advantage #5: You Can Build Your Own Scenarios. 56

Chapter 6: Things to Look Out for in Options Trading 59

Mistake #1: OTM Call Options 60

Mistake #2: Making Misuse of Leverage 61

Mistake #3: Letting Emotions Get the Best of You. 62

Mistake #4: Not Keeping an Open Mind 63

Mistake #5: Dealing with Illiquid Options 64

Mistake #6: Not Buying Back Contracts................ 66

Mistake #7: Not Doing your Homework............... 67

Chapter 7: Making Regular Income from Options Trading 70

Starting Capital Required 71

Income Generated from Options Trading 72

Frequency of Trading 74

Rolling Over Profits 76

Trading in a Band 77

Chapter 8: Profiting from Covered Calls 81

Holding a Long Position 82

How a Covered Call Works 83

Things to Avoid in a Covered Call 87

Don't pledge more stock than you own 87

Don't be afraid to buy it back 88

Don't wait too long 89

Don't make covered calls with highly liquid stocks 90

Chapter 9: Profiting from Naked Puts 92

How a Naked Put Works 93

Things to Look Out for in a Naked Put 97

Chapter 10: How to Short a Stock Using Options . 102

Overview of Shorting Stocks 103

Example of a Short Sale 105

Conclusion 112

Introduction

Welcome to the ultimate guide on options trading. If you are here to learn about how you can achieve the income you have always wanted, then you have come to the right place. For most folks, financial matters seem to be foreign to them. It's no wonder. Most financial experts and gurus try to make it as hard as they possibly can.

Why?

The reason is simple. If the average person feels that financial matters are too hard to understand, they will pay these so-called experts lots of money in fees. That's how stockbrokers and money managers make their living. However, modern technology has enabled the average investor to take control of their investments.

In this book, you will find the keys to using options trading to your advantage. You will discover a treasure trove of information that will enlighten your understanding of the financial world. Moreover, you'll find that learning about financial matters is far easier than you could have imagined. The secret is expressing these ideas in plain language. If you're expecting complicated technical jargon, then you'll be pleased to find this book has none of that. Sure, we'll be talking about financial terminology, but we'll be doing so in a manner that's easily digestible.

So, let's get started on learning everything you need to know to get started in the world of options trading. You'll discover that options have so much more to offer, especially when compared to the traditional stock market. Plus, options give you the freedom to decide when and what to trade. In the end, options give you total control over your investment decisions. You are in full control of where your money goes. More importantly, you will have total control of the profits you make.

Doesn't that sound like something interesting?

The financial world is full of opportunities. So, it's up to you to make the most of it. This book will help you take full advantage of those opportunities. You'll find that getting started in the financial world can be the most rewarding experience in your life. All you need to do is take that first step. Reading this book is the first step in the right direction.

Don't worry if you don't have much experience in the financial world. While you do need to pay careful attention to the way options work, you will see that this book makes everything easy and simple. It doesn't matter if you have or don't have a degree in economics or finance. This book has been written with the average person in mind. Therefore, your willingness to study the topics presented in this book is all you need to be successful. In the end, success boils down to your dedication to learning.

So, what are you waiting for?

Let's get started on learning what options trading is all about. We are certain that you will enjoy reading this book as much as we enjoyed writing it. Ultimately, learning about a new subject is time well spent.

See you on the inside!

Chapter 1
Welcome to Trading Options

If this is the first time you've read about options trading, then sit back and relax. This is an introduction to the world of options trading. In particular, you will find that options trading is based on logic and common sense. By using these elements, you can be successful at making money right from the start.

But first, let's talk about what options are. In essence, options are contracts that two parties make to buy and sell an asset. Now, the term "asset" refers to the object that is traded. This is important to note as the asset in question could be anything. Of course, we're talking about "financial assets." As such, there is a specific number of items at play.

Specifically, stocks are at play in options trading. When you buy and sell stocks, you do so at their current market price. So, if you want to buy or sell a stock on March 15th, you will pay the price of that stock on March 15th.

But what if you could buy or sell the stock on June 10th at March 15th's price?

This is what options are all about.

Options contracts give you the flexibility to negotiate terms and conditions based on any number of parameters. These parameters will determine the nature of the contract. Consequently, you'll have the opportunity to make a profit by taking advantage of these conditions.

It is also worth noting that options contracts provide you with the opportunity to protect yourself against the risk that comes with trading in the stock market. Since the future is uncertain, options give you the chance to protect yourself from any scenario that might unfold. Therefore, options are known to "hedge" against risk. In other words, options help you protect your investments in case things take an unexpected turn.

How Options Work

The way options contracts work is quite straightforward. The two parties that engage in the negotiation agree on the price and timeframe in which stocks are bought or sold. Hence, one party agrees to sell while the other party agrees to purchase.

Now, the reason why they are "options" is because none of the parties are obligated to go through with the deal. Therefore, the buyer or seller has the "option" to go through with the contract. Otherwise, they can let the contract expire without it being used.

Based on this concept, we can infer there are two important parameters, time and price. The time parameter refers to the duration of the agreement. Options contracts can range from a few hours to months. There is no fixed timeframe for options. The time parameter can be set to any time the buyer of the contract sees fit.

The price parameter is the price at which both parties agree to conduct the deal. This is called the "strike price." As such, a strike price refers to the price point at which the buyer and seller agree to make the deal happen. As a result, if the deal is executed, the transaction will occur at the specified price. Moreover, fluctuations in market valuation are meaningless. This implies that whatever the agreed price is, that's what the contract will be based upon.

Also, please note that the buyer of the contract has the option to go through with it or not. When we say the "buyer" of the contract, we're talking about the person who holds the right to the contract. Whether the contract is to buy, or sell is irrelevant. What matters here is the individual who holds the right to the contact itself. This concept means that the contract holder can own the right to buy or sell the stock in question.

If the contract holder chooses to exercise it, the transaction will occur at the specified price point. If the contract holder chooses not to exercise it, they can let the contract expired unutilized. Therefore, the contract expires worthless, that is, with no monetary value attached to it.

Let's take a look at a practical example to highlight the concept of an options contract.

Two parties enter a negotiation. The item in question is a diamond ring. At present, the ring is worth $1,000. The ring's owner is interested in selling it. The other party is interested in buying it at a specified price point. In fact, the buyer would be willing to buy it at a cheaper price point, that is, under $1,000. So, the prospective buyer approaches the ring's owner with a proposition.

The potential buyer will purchase the ring at $900 in one month's time. To seal the deal, both parties enter an options contract. In this arrangement, the potential buyer purchases the contract. The buyer stipulates the conditions while the seller accepts. Under these terms, the ring's owner cannot sell it until after a month. Now, the seller could offer it around and even make deals, but they cannot sell it until the contract expires.

Let's assume that the ring's value shoots up to $1,500 after a couple of weeks. Thus, the buyer sees an opportunity and decides to execute the contract. The ring's owner cannot hike the price of the buyer. After all, that's why the contract was signed.

In this example, the buyer stands to profit as they bought the ring for a price lower than its current market valuation. The buyer could now turn around and sell the ring for a significant profit. By the same token, the seller loses out on the deal as they could have sold it at a higher price point. Yet, they could not do so unless the buyer chose to let the contract expire.

Now, let's assume that the ring's price falls to $850. At this price point, it doesn't make sense for the buyer to purchase the ring at a higher price point. So, the buyer could simply let the contract expire unused.

In this example, the buyer, as the contract holder, can choose to do let the contract go unexercised. The buyer doesn't lose anything except for the premium paid on the contract.

The premium on an options contract is charge by the writer of the contract. The writer is the person who drafts the contract, thereby becoming the counterparty to the contract holder. In this example, the ring's owner would be the writer as they are the one who has to deliver the asset in question. If the contract holder chooses to allow the contract to expire, the writer (seller in this example) makes money as they collected a fee for writing the contract. As such, the only money the buyer would lose is the premium. Please bear in mind that premiums don't have a set point. Premiums can be as low as a few pennies on the dollar value of an asset while climbing to several dollars. This is why the first thing that options traders need to become familiar with is the cost of premiums.

Types of Options

There are two main types of options that you can use to trade stock, or any other financial asset. These are contracts in which both parties agree to trade the asset. Thereafter, the holder of the option can choose to execute the contract or not.

Let's take a look at them.

Call Option

A call option refers to an agreement in which the holder retains the right to buy the stock in question. It is worth mentioning that this does not constitute an obligation for the holder, but it does represent an obligation to the counterparty. This obligation means that if the holder chooses the exercise the contract, then the counterparty must go through with the deal.

The buyer purchases this type of contract in order to lock in the price of a stock at a specified level. The counterparty then "writes" the contract. In other words, the seller of the stock issues the contract. The price at which both parties agree on the deal is the strike price. The contract holder then has the option to execute the contract from the moment the agreement goes into effect until its expiration. When the contract holder chooses to exercise the option, then the seller must be ready to deliver the stock in question.

This opens an interesting point. The seller doesn't necessarily need to have the shares on hand to make the deal. However, they do need to have the shares on hand at the time the contract is exercised. Therefore, the seller must be prepared to furnish the stock at a moment's notice.

In this type of contract, the seller acts as the writer. Thus, they get to collect the premium for the contract itself. Therefore, the buyer must pay this fee regardless of whether the contract is used or not. If the contract is exercised, then the buyer pays the premium plus the cost of the shares.

Put Option

Essentially, a put option is the opposite of a call option. In this type of arrangement, the contract holder owns the stock and is looking to sell. As such, the counterparty becomes the buyer. Therefore, when the contract is exercised, the writer (the buyer in this case) must purchase the shares at the specified share price. This arrangement implies that the buyer must have the funds needed to cover the cost of the shares.

The writer of a put option is entitled to collect the premium. Just like a call option, if the contract goes unutilized, then the writer (buyer) collects the premium, thereby making this profit. If the contract goes through, then the write collects the premium but pays the cost of the shares. Ultimately, the writer benefits because they get a "discount" on the total amount paid for the shares. This works for put options writers as they can purchase shares at a lower price.

It is worth noting that plenty of investors use put options as a hedge against risk. This tactic is used since investors have contracts in place should their shares' prices fall below a specified price point. So, rather than go along for the ride, investors can sell at any point the wish. The use of put options for this purpose is known as "stop-loss." In other words, puts are used to stop losses should prices fall precipitously.

In contrast, puts can also be used as a "take-profit" instrument. In this case, investors choose a point at which they are prepared to sell their stock. Once this price point is triggered, they sell their shares and collect their profit. This is used as a means of ensuring they don't miss their opportunity to sell. Therefore, they "take profit" before a shift in the market reduces their ability to make a profit.

Terms and Conditions

The terms and conditions attached to options are fairly straightforward. They don't generally vary from contract to contract. Thus, the two main parameters are expiration and strike price. To make options work effectively, both buyer and seller must agree on the terms. So, if the writer attempts to dictate their terms, they may find it difficult to find interested parties.

It is also possible for writers to issue a put or call option themselves in hopes that some interested party will purchase it. These cases are quite common. So, options traders search the market for open contracts they can purchase. Contract holders can also sell their rights to another party. In this case, contract holders simply collect the premium they paid on the contract. However, it is quite common to see contract holders take less than what they paid for.

Lastly, there are options contracts known as "exotic" options. These types of agreements are somewhat uncommon as they have unusual stipulations. So, finding a counterparty for these deals may be a bit difficult. For instance, exotic options may have unusually long or short expirations or conditions such as political or economic factors that must be triggered before the contract can be used. These types of contracts serve as insurance in case of extreme situations. The writer can also charge an unusually high premium due to the complexity of the deal.

Chapter 2

How to Profit from Trading Options

Making money from trading options is rather straightforward. However, it largely depends on your understanding of the market. Thus, it is paramount that you get the proper know-how. As you gain more knowledge and experience, you'll be able to make more and more consistent profits.

Now, it's important to note that options naturally lose value over time. This is called "time decay." Therefore, time decay is proportionally inverse to the expiration of the contract. So, options contracts are more valuable the more time have before they expire. The reasoning behind this is that a contract that is very close to expiration does not provide the holder enough time to maneuver. In contrast, a contract that has plenty of time left on it can provide the holder with room to maneuver.

Let's look at an example.

A put option is valued at $100. This option is for 100 shares of a corporation valued at $1 apiece. Please keep in mind that the standard for options contracts is 100-share lots. So, if you wanted to purchase 500 shares, you could take out five 100-share contracts. Since the stock in question is highly coveted, the writer agrees to the deal while charging a premium of $0.10 per share. Thus, the total premium paid would be $10. Additionally, the contract is a one-month expiration.

On day one, the contract is worth $10, that is, the full premium that was paid for it. So, if you wanted to turn around and sell your rights, you could easily collect the $10. But if you decided to sell your rights on day 15, the contract would be worth roughly half of what you paid for it.

How so?

The contract only has half of its term left on it. So, it makes sense for a third party to pay only half of the premium. Now, suppose you tried to sell on day 27 or 28, you could reasonably expect to collect only a fraction of the original premium's value.

This is where savvy options traders can make money.

Savvy options traders like to scour the market to find contracts that are close to expiration. Then, they bid for the rights of the contract at a fraction of the original cost. The angle here is to pick up a cheap contract that provides an opportunity to pick up stock at a price point that's better than its current market valuation.

In the case of a call option, investors might be looking to buy shares at a lower price. However, there are none to be found. So, scouring the market for cheap options are a good alternative. If the opportunity is present, then a deal can be made.

Conversely, an investor might be looking to sell their shares. However, the current market valuation does not seem appealing. Hence, a put option makes sense. The investor purchases the rights to a contract at a reduced price and then sells the stock.

Consequently, time decay opens up the door for options traders to make money in two ways. Let's take the time now to explore these alternatives.

Buy Low, Sell High

In this strategy, investors use options to find shares at the desired price point. This means either taking out the option themselves or finding other parties willing to sell their rights. In either case, investors are looking to pick stocks at a much more favorable price.

Investors approach this strategy in one of two ways. Firstly, they go searching for open contracts on a specific stock. For example, investors search for open contracts on Apple or Microsoft stock. If they find them at their desired price point, they'll scoop them up. Secondly, investors search for open contracts in hopes of finding a good deal. Here, the company itself is not the target. Instead, the target is the contract itself. The company then becomes a secondary target. Naturally, if the company is not worth the risk, then it makes sense to pass on the contract.

So, let's explore how investors stand to profit under this approach.

Scenario #1:

An investor is interested in purchasing stock in a company. This company's current share price sits at

$12.50 per share. As such, the investor looks for options to find a lower price point for the stock. The investor finds an open contract for the stock at $12 per share. The contract has a premium of $5 with 10 days remaining on a 30-day expiration. The investor purchases the rights to the contract for $2. Then, executes the contract. The investor gets the shares at $12 apiece. Then, they turn around and sell the stock at the current market valuation. They profit $0.50 per share minus the cost of the premium.

Scenario #2:

An investor is bargain hunting. They find an option that's about to expire. This is a call on a corporation that is currently valued at $13 a share. The option has a strike price of $12.75. The contract was two days left on its duration. So, the investor scoops up the contract for a fraction of its original value. Since the stock is currently valued above the strike price, the investor sees the potential for a quick profit. So, they scoop up the call paying a modest premium. Then, they immediately exercise the option. Once they have bought the stock at $12.75, they promptly sell at $13. The profit is $0.25 per share minus the premium.

In both of these scenarios, the investor needs to move quickly. The investor is keen on time. They know that acting quickly will maximize gains. Unlike the traditional "buy and hold" strategy, the "buy low, sell high" strategy requires investors to act fact. Otherwise, market shifts may zap their profits altogether. As such, the investor needs to take advantage of an expiring option while also cashing in on the current market valuation.

Using Options for Speculative Purposes

In the stock market, speculative is like gambling. Investors make bets on what they hope will or will not happen. In such cases, investors can use options contracts to place their bets. Options provide investors with the opportunity to make risky deals without exposing themselves to unwanted consequences.

Speculation consists of what you, as an investor, believe will happen even when you are not sure, if or when it will actually take place. When speculators hit a home run, they clean up. When they strike out, they can be wiped out.

Let's consider an example.

A corporation's stock is currently trading at $16 a share. Historically, this company's stock has traded between $14 to $17 a share. However, investors are anticipating a breakout as the company is set to unveil a new product line. If all goes well, the company's stock will soar. As such, investors are looking to get in now before the stock takes off for the moon.

So, investors are prepared to get in now. However, there is no telling when the price will take off. Buying the stock now and waiting for it to take off would imply using the buy and hold strategy. However, investors are never willing to tie up their money for longer than absolutely necessary. Consequently, investors can use options to both buy and sell stocks.

In this example, an investor can use a combination of call and put options. For example, the investor can use a call option to buy the stock at $16 and sell at $20. But here's the tricky part. It is unclear when the stock will take off, and most importantly, it is not clear if the stock will take off at all.

A savvy speculator purchases the options contracts to ensure that they will hedge their position. That way, they won't commit their money without being sure of what will happen. If the stock doesn't take off, the investor doesn't have to exercise any of the options. If anything, they will simply lose the money on the premiums. This is a small change compared to getting wiped out on a downturn. However, if the deal goes as expected, the profits will easily offset the cost of the contracts.

This is the reason why speculators live and die by their options. Since they clearly understand the way that options work, they can leverage them to their advantage. Moreover, if you plan to plan the speculation game, then you must use options in your favor. Otherwise, using the buy and hold strategy on long shots will cause you to miss a great deal of opportunities. It is worth noting that the buy and hold strategy is great for blue-chip stocks, that is, companies that are certain to perform at or beyond expectations. Since these stocks are highly coveted, you can be sure that you can sell them at any time. Thus, they are the closest thing you'll find to a sure bet. Anything that isn't considered as blue-chip would best be treated as a speculative investment. Therefore, options must become your go-to option.

Writing Contracts

Writing options contracts is an alternative best employed by seasoned traders. The reason for this is that writers must have stock and/or cash on hand. Writing options can be attractive for investors and traders as most contracts often you unused. This means that you can basically keep the premium contract holders pay. However, you cannot assume that the contract will go unused. You must always assume the contract will be used. That way, you need to be ready. Otherwise, you'll run into trouble.

There are two ways in which you can make money as an options writer. The first is to agree with another party beforehand. That way, you draft up the contract based on the specific agreement you have with the counterparty. This type of arrangement is quite common with exotic options. The second way is to write up a contract and put it out there. That way, other investors can come along and buy it from you. To make that work, you need to look for the right terms. Often that means making the contract attractive so that other traders find value in it.

For example, you are holding stock in a corporation. As such, you are looking to sell it. In that case, you can write a call option. A buyer that's interested in purchasing stock in that corporation will find it and buy the rights. If the premium you have assigned makes sense to the buyer, then you have a deal. If the buyer exercises the contract, then you make the transaction.

So, please bear in mind that when you write the contract, you don't have the right to exercise it. You sell that right to the other party. That's why you can't assume that it won't be exercised. You must always assume it will be.

Also, you can write a put option. In this case, you are looking to buy stock in a company. You write up the contract and then an interested party will buy the rights. That gives them the option to sell you the stock if they choose to. That means you must be ready to pay for the stock in case the contract is exercised.

Now, the biggest question is what premium should you charge?

There are two answers to that question.

First of all, you can charge whatever the market going rate is. All you have to do is look for similar options and see what the premiums are. You can then determine where you want to set your target. You could charge slightly less in order to draw attention. You could also charge slightly more if you feel that you have better terms.

Next, you could offer a discounted premium. While this may be frowned upon by some traders, it's a great way for newbies to get their foot in the door. Now, if you are holding stock of a highly coveted company, you could practically charge whatever you want so long as it is within reason. In the end, you are free to set your premiums based on what your contract has to offer.

Chapter 3
How to Trade Call and Put Options

Making money with options goes beyond the mere act of buying and selling the underlying stocks. When you deal with options, there are a number of ways in which you can make money. As such, you need to learn how options themselves can make you money, especially when market conditions aren't all that favorable. Moreover, you will be surprised to find that you can make money with options even in the worst of market conditions. All you need to do is be keen on how they work. So, while others are losing money, you can make a profit. In the end, you profit while others are heading for the hills.

In this chapter, we are going to be looking at how you can trade calls and puts. This means that you can trade the contracts themselves. Plus, you can take advantage of the demand created by other investors' trades and transactions. In the end, you can certainly make money when you are clear on how options work.

Buying an Options Contract

It is important to note that when you buy an options contract, you are buying the right to the contract. It doesn't matter whether you are buying or selling the stock itself. What you are acquiring when you purchase the contract is the right to exercise the deal. Therefore, you are acquiring a right that you can choose to utilize or not.

There are two main ways in which you can buy an option.

One, you can buy an existing contract. You can choose any options so long as it is up for sale. Thus, contract holders will place their contracts on the open market. This gives contract holders the flexibility to either exercise the contract or sells it to whoever is interested in purchasing it. In some cases, contract holders will place their options on the market as they approach expiration. The reasoning here is that someone who is in desperate need may choose to scoop it up. It makes sense for the contract holder to do so because they can recoup a part of the original premium they paid for the contract. While they may not recover the entire sum they paid, they will at least get something back.

A good place to find existing options contracts is Barchart. Barchart is an exchange service in which you can buy and sell options contracts. Also, it is a great place for you to get an idea of the premiums paid for the various types of options available. This is a great research tool, especially if you are thinking about becoming a writer. That way, you can gain insight into how much you can charge for writing an option.

It is worth noting that contract holders usually take out contracts for the hottest stocks. They do so because they know that investors are always looking to find shares for these companies. That's why having an options contract makes the most sense. It is a way in which they can assure themselves that they'll get the shares they need when they need them.

Another interesting angle is that when stockbrokers and investors make deals, they don't necessarily need to deliver the shares they sold. They can deliver an options contract. The reason why stockbrokers can do this is that an options contract is as good as the stock itself. In the event that one of the parties in the agreement is unable to uphold their end, the contract holder can demand indemnity for the damage caused. In the end, the contract holder doesn't stand to lose.

Two, you can create a new contract. This is when two parties willingly engage in an agreement. As such, both parties agree on the terms and conditions of the deal. In the end, they write up their contract, and that is that. It is worth noting that most of these contracts don't make it to a public screener like Barchart. While they might, it is rare. Still, as you get to know other investors, you might be presented with opportunities such as these, especially if you are prepared to write the contract. These types of contracts don't often get sold, particularly if the conditions stipulate some kind of prohibition. Nevertheless, you could sell them with the consent of the counterparty.

It is also worth mentioning that the writer of the contract cannot sell their side of the options contract. The reason for this lies in the fact that the writer does not hold any rights. The writer is obligated to go through with the agreement when the rightsholder chooses to exercise them. As such, the writer is under obligation and therefore cannot sell their participation in the contract.

Selling an Options Contract

In this scenario, selling a contract means selling the rights to the contract whether it's a call or a put. As such, the seller already holds the rights to a contract. Therefore, they have the choice to sell their rights, particularly if there is an interested third party looking to buy the underlying stock.

Let's take a look at the reasons why you would see an options contract.

Firstly, let's assume you are holding a call option for a company. Since you are holding a call, you have the right to purchase the stock specified in the contract. Consequently, your rights enable you to acquire the stock at any point during the validity period of the contract.

Now, let's assume that there is another investor who is in need of purchasing the same company's stock. This investor may have a hard time finding shares available on the market or might be exercising caution in a deal. Consequently, this investor is looking to get their hands on the stock. If the stock is unavailable in liquid form, that is other investors that are willing to sell straight up, then the next best alternative is to buy an existing call option. This assures the investor the stock they need.

So, here is how the contract holder can make money. If the stock is in short supply, the contract holder can hike the premium on the contract. For example, the contract holder paid a $10 premium for the contract. But since the stock is in short supply, other desperate investors may be willing to pay $15 or $20 for the contract itself. This happens frequently when the agreements have a much lower strike price as compare to the current market valuation. At this point, the contract holder sells and makes a profit.

Secondly, you are holding the rights to a put option. These types of agreements are in high demand when the price of a stock tanks. When this occurs, stockholders are left scrambling to sell. Fearing they might get wiped out, they are willing to pay anything to secure a better sale price. This is where contract holders can make a good chunk of change. When desperate stockholders are seeking a better deal, puts can shoot up in value. This occurs when puts have a significantly higher strike price than the current market valuation.

For example, a company's stock is currently valued at $11 a share. This is significantly lower than its former $14 high. Plenty of investors got in at this price point. However, the stock's valuation has sunk. Now, stockholders are desperately looking to cut their losses. So, puts for this stock are in high demand. Any contract over $11 a share is highly coveted. So, holders of these puts can command any price they way on the premium. Naturally, the increase needs to be reasonable. Otherwise, investors might as well absorb the loss.

Another reason puts become highly coveted in when no one wants a particular stock. This generally occurs when companies run into trouble. As such, investors shy away from purchasing that company's stocks. So, stockholders are stuck with shares that nobody wants. This is where a put option can become quite popular. Investors that are stuck with bad shares can purchase the puts and dump the stock. It affects the writer, but such is the risk for the contract writer.

Lastly, both calls and puts can be quite lucrative with investors that short stocks. A short sale is when an investor sells a stock they do not own. Consequently, the first pledge the shares and then must buy them. In a successful short sale, the short seller sells the stock first, receives the proceeds, and then must find the same shares at a lower price.

This is where options come into play. The contract holder can profit from the short seller's urgent need by hiking the premium. If the short seller is in a real pinch, they might be willing to pay just about anything.

Another angle to this scenario is writing a contract specifically for the short seller. Let's assume that you happen to hold shares in that specific stock. So, you write a call in which you pledge your shares. The short seller is fortunate to find the shares at a decent price. And while the premium might be higher than usual, you profit by selling the shares and collecting the premium.

Using Options to Invest with Little Money

One of the most attractive features of options trading is that you can invest in them with very little money. This is why options are great for investors that are just starting out and don't have much investment capital.

Let's look at an example of how this works.

An investor has $300 to invest. This investor is looking to purchase shares of a corporation valued at $9 apiece. If the investor took the $300 and bought shares straight up, that would only get them 33 or so of that company's stock. If the corporation's valuation rose to $10, that would mean an income of $330. The investor's gross profit would be $30.

Now, let's consider how the investor can use options to multiply their earnings.

The investor purchases two contracts for the same corporation. The investor purchases one call and one put. In general, all options contracts are for 100-share blocks. So, if the investor purchases a call option, they would really be in line to purchase 100 shares of the corporation. Of course, if the investor chooses to exercise the call option, they will have to pay $900 for the stock.

Here's the trick, though.

By purchasing the contract, the investor only has to pay the premium and not the share's value. So, the investor pays $150 for the premium of the call option. Then, the investor pays another $150 for the premium on a put option. The call option has a strike valuation of $90 a share while the put option has a price of $100 a share.

To make the deal work, the investor exercises the put option first, receives the proceeds, and then exercises the call option. They receive the shares from the call option and deliver them to the buyer in the put option.

Let's take a look at the profit.

Put option: 100 shares @ $100 apiece = $10,000.

Call option: 100 shares @ $90 apiece = $9,000.

Gross profit: $1,0000 - $9000 = $1000.

As you can see, the investor made $1000 in profit while investing only $300. In this example, the investor made a gross profit of $1,000 on the difference between stock prices. Now, we have to discount the premium paid on both contracts, that is, $300. So, $1,000 - $300 = $700. In total, the investor made a profit of $700 while investing only $300. In this scenario, the investor more than doubled their money.

The difference between the profits in the first example and the second one is abysmal. The reason for this lies in the fact that options enable you to use leverage. In other words, you can buy into stocks that you wouldn't otherwise afford. This is because you are only purchasing the rights to the stocks and not the stocks themselves.

Chapter 4

Making Money in a Bull or Bear Market

Investors live and die by the words "bear" or "bull." These terms are used to refer to the state of the stock market. They are also consistently thrown around in the media. Whenever investors, or the average person, hears any of these words, their minds suddenly go into overdrive.

In the worst of cases, investors are wrought with fear. Fear then leads to panic. This is where you see stockbrokers losing their shirts over a bad deal they made when times were good. Also, panic leads the average investor to cash out their investment accounts leaving them in the hole.

So, what is a "bull" or "bear" market?

In this chapter, we are going to define these terms while discussing how you can make money regardless of market conditions. This means that you won't have to worry about the state of the market. When you know how to use options to your advantage, all you need to do is search for the right deals. Then, you just need to pull the trigger.

Defining a Bull Market

Let's start with the good times. A bull market is a designation given to a trend that indicates stock prices are rising. In this scenario, the overall valuation of the market is rising. As such, optimism takes over the minds of investors leading them to be more willing to invest.

Analysts sanction a bull market following a recession. When economists finally declare that a recession is over, investors and market analysts look for a sustained trend of rising stock prices. When the market's overall valuation reaches the same point at which a recession was declared, analysts will then declare the beginning of a new bull market.

It is worth noting that a bull market is a speculative term. Sure, the data point toward the market gaining in valuation. However, it is a subjective appreciation as more cautious investors may choose to wait even longer to declare a bull market.

The main characteristic of a bull market is that investors tend to feel more optimistic. When optimism reigns, investors are much more willing to take risks. This implies a willingness to buy more stocks. Overall, this trend leads to stock prices to gain more and more value. This is a bull market that tends to drive prices upward. Of course, the upward trend is not across the board. After all, there are companies that still lose money during a bull market. Still, the overall trend is a positive one.

It is also worth noting that there are drivers of a bull market. These drivers are stocks that gain an enormous amount. As such, they tend to pull most of the weight in the market. To put this point into perspective, the stock market's general value is calculated as the average of all stocks. So, there are winners and losers. The average valuation of all stocks yields a positive value during a bull market.

The best part of a bull market is that it's not hard to find profitable stocks. During a bull market, a good number of stocks make money. Sure, some make more than others. However, that is a secondary point. It's also important to consider that making huge gains in a bull market is also quite possible. It's common to find significant jumps in stock valuations. Savvy investors know when to spot potential breakouts. That's where options can help set them up for the big moves.

Seasoned options traders know that a bull market means that they need to cash in as much as possible. This is quite feasible with the right stocks. These profits can help them prepare for the winter, that is when the bear market pops in for a visit.

Defining a Bear Market

A bear market is the opposite of a bull market. This occurs when there is a generalized decrease in the market's valuation. This calculation is the result of averaging out the earnings of all stocks. If the end calculation is negative, then the market is sustaining losses.

Generally speaking, analysts declare a bear market when it falls 20% from its previous highs. A 10% falls means the market is going through a correction. The term "correction" means that the market is simply recalculating value as it attempts to find stability. The reasoning for these correction lies in the psyche of investors. When investors feel that stocks are too expensive, they begin to pull their money. Consequently, they may choose to invest their fund in other asset classes or investment instruments. These shifts in investors' psyche leads the market to recalculate its valuation.

Still, corrections are normal. For investors that don't anticipate corrections, they can get stuck in a tough spot. This is where options can provide a way out of a jam. Savvy investors know that a bear market is always around the corner. So, they make the most of options by hedging their positions. Ultimately, they can use options to protect their positions, especially when engaging in riskier trades.

A bear market is nothing to be afraid of. For experienced investors, they know that bear markets are not the end of the world. Moreover, their experience teaches them how to prepare for such times. Also, having experience with bear markets provides investors with the means to make money when others panic.

That's why options are the most important investment vehicle you could dabble in. However, the media and so-called "gurus" would much rather you didn't invest in options.

How so?

If everyone invested in options, then the playing field would be much more level. Since most folks ignore the virtues of investing in options, they opt for the "buy and hold" strategy. Needless to say, this strategy benefits stockbrokers and investment banks, but not the investors themselves.

Now, if you are content with putting your money into an account every month and simply forgetting about it, then they buy and hold strategy would be a good alternative for you. This strategy makes a lot of sense if you have a lot of time ahead of you. For example, younger investors can certainly benefit from this approach.

Additionally, the buy and hold strategy is ideal for passive investors. In short, a passive investor is the type of person who does not want to be actively involved in their investment decisions. They would much rather leave that up to a fund manager. However, this doesn't sound like you since you are taking the time to read this book. Therefore, you sound like the active investor type. So, do read on.

How to Make Money During a Bull Market

Making money in a bull market is much easier than doing so in a bear market. Since most investors are feeling optimistic, they are much more willing to risk money. This is where options can help you cash in as investors pour it on.

Generally speaking, investors that ride out a bear market find a bull market as the opportunity to cash out of their positions. This occurs as investors recoup the losses they suffered during the downturn. This means that there are plenty of sellers. This situation implies that it's also a good time to be a buyer.

In this scenario, you can use call options to help you lock in good share prices, especially when prices are going up across the board. So, you can lock in prices before they shoot up. In doing so, you can ensure that you have a chance to sell the stock at a much higher profit.

Please note that this move is highly useful as you are not subject to market fluctuations. By using calls, you can ensure that you will get the stock you seek at the right price. Essentially, you're taking the guesswork out of making trades.

During a bull market, put options become a significant tool. You can use options to lock in take-profit points, thereby ensuring your profitability. Of course, in a bull market, prices are constantly going up. But you can't assume that they will go up. So, what a put option does is ensure that you will at least make a specific profit. If the price of the stock shoots past your take-profit point, you can always sell at that higher point.

This is the beauty of options contracts.

It's also worth noting that during a bull market, trading activity tends to pick up. So, there are always investors looking to purchase stock, particularly in hot companies. If you can line up contracts in companies that are highly sought-after, you can simply turn around and sell those contracts for a profit. The key here is to find companies that investors want. That way, your contracts will be highly attractive. If you choose to write to them, you can command a higher premium. That alone generates more profit, especially when compared to regular buy and sell trades.

Making Money in a Bear Market

Making money during good times seems pretty straightforward. However, making money during tough times isn't always easy. In fact, most investors head for the hills whenever a bear market looms. This means that there is a massive selloff. This is a bargain-hunting season for a lot of investors. As such, many investors wait for desperate stockholders to sell off their shares at whatever price they can get.

While buying at extremely low market valuations makes sense, the problem is that such stocks may not necessarily bounce back, at least not in the short term. This is why put options make a great deal of sense.

When prices are dropping all around, put options to protect stockholders against sinking prices. In general, stockholders find that obtaining put options gives them a sense of ease. The reason for this lies in knowing they can dump their shares in case the price tanks. Unfortunately, the counterparty is then stuck with stock that's quickly losing value.

As an investor, you can use puts to protect your investment, particularly when there is a chance that prices may fall.

For example, you are holding stock in a company whose current valuation is $9 a share. You take out an option at that valuation to protect yourself just in case. You are really hoping for the price to go up. But should it fall, you'll be ready for it. Now, let's assume that the price fell to $8 apiece. You can exercise your put in this case.

As for calls, you can use them to pick up stock at good prices in case prices rebound. This is an important point to consider. During bear markets, investors are constantly trying to find the bottom of the market. This means that investors try to anticipate the lowest point in the market. Knowing when the bottom will hit is significant as prices rebound following the bottom. So, it's not uncommon to find spikes in prices throughout a bear market. However, these prices quickly fall back down. Amid these spikes, calls can help you keep your trades in order. Calls can help you avoid having to pay more for stocks. What's worse, you may find that prices suddenly fall back down after you have made a purchase at a higher price point. Therefore, having an option makes more sense.

The biggest advantage that options provide you during a bear market is certainty. Certainty is crucial during uncertain times. This is painfully evident during bear markets as no one can tell exactly how low prices can fall. While falling prices are great for buyers, they can be disastrous for sellers. By the same token, you might miss an opportunity as a buyer if you're not ready. By having options agreements in place, you can ensure that you won't miss opportunities. In some cases, you may not even need to exercise your rights. But should things take an unexpected turn, you'll be ready to make the necessary moves.

So, don't be afraid of bear markets. By using options to your advantage, you can leverage any situation in your favor.

Chapter 5

How to Manage Risk in Options Trading

Risk is an inherent part of stock trading. Any time you choose to put money into financial markets, you are opening the door for a series of potential issues. Naturally, it's not always easy to invest in stocks. Now, most financial advisors or stockbrokers will have you think that there is nothing you can do to protect yourself against risk. This is true if you are a passive investor. Passive investors can't really do much but go along for the ride. In such cases, the best that investors can hope for is to ride the storm and recoup their losses during a bull market.

So, let's take a look at why this strategy is highly flawed.

Long-term investing makes you vulnerable as you can't really do much to protect against market fluctuations. Investors can only hope that the overall valuation of their portfolio will not get hammered whenever there is a recession or bear market.

The risk management strategy that stockbrokers sell their customers is diversification. Diversification means that a client's portfolio is spread across various stocks and asset classes. This strategy is meant to offset the losses from one stock with the gains from another. However, this strategy fails when there is a decline across the board.

To make matters worse, older investors don't have the luxury of riding out downturns in the market. Older investors, particularly those close to retirement age, may not be able to afford to retire during a market downturn. This is why passive investing is better suited for younger investors who do have the luxury of time.

Seasoned investors and traders know that the best way they can hedge against risk is to use options. Options take the guesswork out of investing. As such, traders use options to their advantage. However, they won't share that advantage with their clients.

Do you see an unfair pattern, here?

This is why this chapter is about showing you how you can use options to protect you against market downturns. Options can also set you up for riding the wave of market upswings. Either way, options help you protect yourself from unexpected events. That way, you won't have to lose any sleep over your investments.

Advantage #1: Locking in Prices

When you take out an options contract, you lock in prices. Options enable you to predetermine price points. As such, market fluctuations don't affect the valuation of your stocks. Moreover, they can help you make good deals even if the markets suddenly hit a snag.

By the same token, you can lock in prices when you see that stocks are poised to shoot through the roof. Consequently, you can protect yourself against a sudden spike. So, let's take a look at how you can protect yourself.

You currently hold stock in a corporation. This corporation's current valuation sits at $12 a share. You purchased the stock at $11 a share. At this point, you are making a $1 profit on each share. However, you are unsure about how the stock will perform down the road. So, you take out a put option at $12 a share. While you are not looking to sell right now, you are prepared to do if the stock's valuation falls below $11.

Now, it's important to consider this point as you may not be able to sell your shares when the price falls through the floor. You might be willing to take $11 just to break even. However, other investors may not be willing to pay that much. Having a put option ensures that you don't get fleeced should the price fall through the floor.

Advantage #2: Cash Is King

Now, it's always important to remember that cash is king. Thus, liquidity is the name of the game when it comes to investing. Unprepared investors find that when they need money the most, they are unable to sell their shares.

Let's look at an example.

An investor needs funds to cover a payment. However, they are short on cash. This means that the only alternative they have is to liquidate stock in order to cover the payments. Since the investor is unprepared, they have a hard time finding a buyer for their stock. In particular, they find it hard to find an investor at the price point they want. This means the investor either liquidates the stock for less than anticipated, or they must find another way to come up with the funds they need.

Can you see the complication, here?

A prepared investor would have a put option in place for their holdings. It is highly useful to have open contracts on their holdings as this would protect them against the need to cover liabilities. As such, whenever an investor needs to cover a liability, they are prepared to liquidate stock on short notice.

Please keep in mind that having cash on hand is always key. There are times when investors need funds to pounce on a great opportunity. So, having open options enables them to move quickly. Otherwise, their reaction time may be too slow. In that case, it may lead them to missed opportunities.

Advantage #3: Ensuring Profits

Unpredictability is one of the overarching themes in this book. Even when markets are rocking, there is no telling what can happen. That is why options can be used to filter out potential surprises. These surprises can be quite annoying when they zap your profits.

Shifts in markets can happen very quickly. These shifts can lead you to see your profits dwindle or disappear altogether. As such, having open options on hand is a great way of managing the situation in your favor.

Let's consider this scenario.

You hold stock in a company whose valuation sits at $13 a share. You are prepared to purchase at this price point as you anticipate the stock's valuation to rise. This opens the door to risk. After all, there is no telling if the price will go up. While you may have a reasonable assumption that the price will go up, it's not something you can bet your life on. Moreover, if prices do go up, there is no telling how high they can go.

So, you decide to take a put option at $15 a share. This option protects you in two ways.

First, this contract locks in a price point that is favorable in case the stock doesn't rise or falls. You can sell your stock at this price point and collect your earnings. The counterparty is then left to take on the stock they pledged.

Second, this put option helps you manage your profits in case you don't have enough time to react. For instance, let's assume that the stock has hit $15 a share. However, you anticipate that the stock may go even higher. In that case, $16 seems like a reasonable possibility. However, the stock doesn't go up that high. Moreover, there is a real possibility that it might fall back down under $15 a share. Having the open contract gives you peace of mind in knowing that you already have an advantageous position on hand. Thus, you can afford to wait and see how things will play out without running the risk of losing money.

Advantage #4: Options Buy You Time

Time is of the essence of investing. For most investors, time is not a luxury they can afford. Many times, investors find that time is working against them. This is why options give you the luxury of time. So long as an agreement is valid, you can afford to wait and see how things unfold.

Let's look at how you can use a call option to buy you time.

During earnings season, companies must report their financial statements. At this point, companies can either fall short or exceed expectations. Depending on the result, prices can jump or fall. For this particular corporation, analysts expect it to show positive earnings. However, it is unknown how positive the results will be.

Consequently, you are looking to ride the wave but don't really know how far could rise. However, you are not keen on purchasing the stock straight up as you are not willing to take on any unnecessary risk. Therefore, you choose to purchase a call option.

The stock's current valuation sits at $8 a share. However, buying the stock now would mean tying up your cash until the earnings announcement is made. Since you are unsure how much the price would go up, then a call makes the most sense.

Now, the company has announced its earnings. They have exceeded expectations. Overnight, the stock shoots up to $10 a share. You can breathe easy as you have a contract on hand. You can exercise the contract, purchase the stock at $8 apiece, and then turn around to sell it at $10 a share.

Do you see how the contract buys you time in this case?

Additionally, you don't even need to use up any of your own funds to make this deal work. You could pledge the stock at $10, receive the proceeds and then exercise the call at $8. That way, you receive the stock that you must furnish to your buyer.

As you can see, options can buy you time. This is a luxury that is highly coveted by investors. Nevertheless, very few investors know how to use options for this purpose.

Advantage #5: You Can Build Your Own Scenarios

We have often mentioned how options can help you avoid falling prey to market fluctuations. As such, options allow you to control your destiny. This is what we mean when we say that you can build your own scenarios.

Let's take a look at how you can build your own scenario using a combination of options.

A company is currently trading at $50 a share. This is a record high for this company. So, it's reasonable to assume that the company's share price would fall. However, you also believe that it's plausible for the price to keep climbing. But there is no real way of telling what will happen.

To build your own scenario, you assume that the price will continue to climb but you also assume the price will fall. This enables you to get two options. You purchase a call option at $47 a share while you write a call option at $52 share.

In the first call option, you are purchasing the right to buy the stock at a price point of $47. If the price falls below $47, then there would be no need to exercise the contract. Should the price continue to climb, you have a contract that puts you in a great spot.

In the second call option, you are the writer. So, if the contract holder exercises the option, you are forced to sell the stock at $52. The only catch to this situation is that you would need to furnish the stock should the option be exercised.

Now, let's assume the price keeps climbing. The share price is not at $55 a share. The holder of the second contract exercises it at $52. Immediately, you exercise your call at $47. You buy at $47 and sell at $52. Automatically, you make a $5 profit on each share. Plus, you may even be able to get the premiums to offset each other since you paid the premium on one contract but collected it on the other.

Now, let's assume the price falls to $45 a share. The holder of the second option will not exercise their option at $52. Also, you wouldn't exercise yours at $47. As such, both options would go unused. Still, you wouldn't stand to lose any money as the premiums on both contracts would offset one another. Therefore, this is a no harm, no foul situation. Conversely, you might even profit from this deal if the counterparty on the contract you wrote paid a higher premium than you did for the first call.

As you can see, options are a fantastic way of helping you manage your destiny.

Chapter 6

Things to Look Out for in Options Trading

When starting out with options trading, it's important to be on the lookout for some common mistakes that novice traders make. These mistakes are easily avoidable. However, they require you to pay attention to them. That way, you can steer clear from running into trouble. Unfortunately, some traders find out about these mistakes a little too late. That is why it's crucial that you keep an eye out for them. In doing so, you'll save yourself a number of headaches down the road.

In this chapter, we are going to be looking at the major mistakes that options traders make when going about their new trading endeavors. So, please take the time to go over each one of these points. That way, you can save yourself time, trouble, and money by avoiding them altogether.

Mistake #1: OTM Call Options

An OTM call option (out of the money) means that the option is set up for the purchase of a stock whose valuation is higher on the contract that its current market valuation. In other words, the contract is set up to purchase a stock at a higher price than it's truly worth.

These types of options abound. While such contracts are not a mistake in themselves, they are a problem for holders. Consider this example.

A trader holds a call option for a company for $10 a share. However, this company's current valuation sits at $9. So, it wouldn't make any sense to exercise the contract as you would be paying more than if you just bought on the open market.

Do you see the mistake here?

Now, because this option is OTM, it is much cheaper. Therefore, it may seem like an attractive offer. It's one thing to take a flyer on an option such as this, especially if you believe the stock's price will rebound. In such a case, you would get a steal.

The problem with this strategy is that if you consistently purchase OTM options, you'll essentially throw your money away. Even if you do get them very cheaply, purchasing them on a regular basis will add up. In a way, it's like buying a lottery ticket. So, it's best to stay away from OTM calls unless you have a reasonable belief the stock will bounce back.

Mistake #2: Making Misuse of Leverage

Options offer a great deal of leverage. As seen earlier, you don't need to have the cash on hand to buy the shares pledged in a call option. As long as you hold the contract, you practically own the shares. However, the problem lies when you actually need to purchase the shares. In this case, you need to be sure that you can produce the funds to cover the cost of the call option.

Consider this situation.

You purchase three calls at $50 a share. Assuming each contract is for 100 shares apiece, you're on the hook for 300 shares should you choose to exercise the contract. If you own the call and don't have the money to cover the purchase, then you simply let the contract expire. However, you would be throwing your money away for nothing. This is why calls can be purchased quite easily. There are investors who run into trouble. So, they would rather sell their rights for whatever they can get.

It is wise to engage in deals that you know you can cover. For instance, you can liquate other stocks or have some reserves you can draw from. This is why the most recommended course of action early on is to only trade one contract at a time. That way, you won't run the risk of running into trouble. As you build your investment capital and trading acumen, you can gradually engage in larger and larger deals.

Mistake #3: Letting Emotions Get the Best of You

The phrase, "cut your losses" is the most important investment advice you will hear. When deals don't work out, savvy traders know they need to pull the plug as soon as possible. However, novice traders are always tempted to wait a little bit longer. The problem with waiting too long is that your losses may pile up in a hurry. Consequently, you'll find yourself struggling to get back on track.

When you find that an option you hold is OTM, be it a call or a put, it's best to dump it. Even if you take a hit on the premium, it's preferable to recoup something rather than lose everything. That way, you can essentially live to fight another day.

Another important action to avoid is "doubling down." Doubling down consists of doubling your next trade in hopes of recouping what you lost on the previous one. The fact is that this strategy seldom works. If anything, it often leads investors to double down on their losses. It's a strategy that poses an unnecessary risk. So, it's always a good idea to stay the course. You will eventually break even as the profits from other deals offset the losses of others.

Mistake #4: Not Keeping an Open Mind

All too often, investors and traders get caught up in a single strategy. This generally occurs when traders find a solid strategy. Now, we're not saying that you should flipflop from strategy to strategy. What we are saying is that you should always keep your eyes and ears open for new strategies. Who knows, you could uncover a new strategy that could very well complement what you are already doing. Moreover, there could be a better strategy out there.

To implement a new strategy, please be sure to test it out first. You can try it with minimal investment and take it from there. If it works, you can gradually up the ante. If it doesn't, then you can always reflect on why it didn't work. If you feel you can correct mistakes, then try it again. If it doesn't work, then you can forget about it entirely.

Just one word of caution.

Beware of all those so-called experts out there who claim they have a foolproof system. Please note that no one has a system that works 100% of the time. In the best of cases, they'll be right 60% or even 70% of the time. These are incredible odds. So, be prepared to miss on some and hit a home run on others. Otherwise, don't pay any attention to anyone claiming they have a foolproof formula or system.

Mistake #5: Dealing with Illiquid Options

In the world of finance, liquidity is one of the most prized assets. In short, liquidity refers to the cash you have on hand, or your ability to get cash in a short time.

Savvy investors know that having some cash on hand is crucial to making good deals happen. Also, savvy traders know that having highly liquid assets can make the difference between making profitable deals for missing opportunities.

Liquid options refer to those contracts which you can quickly sell. Now, it should be noted that it's not the contract itself that's liquid. Instead, it's the underlying stock that makes it liquid. For example, if you have options for stocks such as Google, Apple, or Microsoft, the likelihood of selling them quickly is quite high. Conversely, if you have options based on poorly performing companies, the likelihood of selling them quickly is slimmer.

It's important to keep this in mind as there are times when you might need to come up with cash on short notice. So, having liquid assets makes it much easier to come up with the cash you need. However, if you're holding illiquid assets, you may have a hard time selling. This can be disastrous, especially if you need to cover debts or margin calls. So, always do your homework on the underlying stock. If you're prepared to let your money sit for the duration of the contract, then it's fine.

Otherwise, always make sure you can deal with your options on short notice.

Mistake #6: Not Buying Back Contracts

Options writers often find themselves in a short position, that is, in need to furnish stocks they don't currently own. This means having to come up with the shares when the contract is exercised. On the surface, that's a big problem as it might imply having to go out and find other contracts to cover short positions.

When options writers find themselves in a short position, it might make sense to buy the contract back. That way, they eliminate their short position. Buying back a contract that you've issued might seem counterintuitive. After all, it would essentially mean refunding your customer. However, it makes sense, especially when you can't cover the short position. The inability to cover a short position can happen for a myriad of reasons. Therefore, you should never be afraid to go out and buy back contracts you've written. That way, you can avoid running into trouble down the road.

Consider this situation.

You wrote a call option for a company's stock. The buyer of the option has the right to buy the shares specified in the agreement. Now, let's assume that you don't currently own the stock. That would mean going out to get a call option of your own to cover your short position. However, there are no shares to be found for this company. If the contract you wrote gets exercised, you'll be in trouble. You may be forced to buy the shares at the market price. That might also mean taking a significant hit. To avoid being hit with an uncovered position, you can take a proactive step and buy the contract back. In essence, you are refunding your customer. Still, this is preferable to get hit with a position you cannot cover. So, don't be afraid to buy back a contract you wrote, especially if it will save you plenty of trouble down the road.

Mistake #7: Not Doing your Homework

One of the most important factors in successful trading is doing your homework. By "homework," we're talking about doing research on the markets and individual stocks. This research consists of reading about companies and market trends. As such, you can gain insight into what potential events may occur.

Ultimately, it will give you an idea of what you can expect moving forward.

Throughout this book, we've talked about how options can help you hedge risk. Therefore, your ability to foresee specific events. For instance, it's earnings seasons. So, companies are expected to fall short, meet, or exceed analysts' expectations. Consequently, this would be a perfect time to hold an option in case anything should happen. So, failure to factor an earnings report may lead you to miss an opportunity.

Consider this situation.

A company's current share price stands at $12 apiece. Analysts are expecting it to exceed market expectations. Therefore, it's logical to assume the share price will jump. So, purchasing a call option with a $12 strike price makes sense. Should the price jump over $12 a share, you can buy the stock at a much lower rate. Ultimately, you can go ahead and sell the stock for a considerable profit.

In this example, you won't miss an opportunity by not holding an option that locks in a lower price. In the end, you could always let the contract expire, or sell it off, in case the stock does not perform as expected.

Please keep in mind that the mistakes outlined in this chapter are psychological in nature. Thus, it's always important to keep your eye on the ball and your emotions out of the game. Investors that get caught up in their emotions often lose money. This is the reason why you should try to maintain a level head at all times. Most importantly, being able to cut your losses early on can make a significant difference in your overall performance. So, don't be afraid to act. Taking decisive action can mean the difference between getting or staying out of trouble.

Chapter 7

Making Regular Income from Options Trading

The vast majority of folks that get into options trading do so as a means of supplementing their income. Some "gurus" out there claim that you can make a living by trading options. On the surface, this is plausible. However, it largely depends on how much money you need to truly make a living from options trading.

So, most investors look at options as a means of making regular income, thereby supplementing other trading, investing, or job-related activities. Therefore, it's perfectly reasonable to assume you can supplement your monthly income right from the start. But please keep in mind that making substantial gains depends on your level of expertise, experience, and commitment to trading. Casual investors and traders don't make nearly as much money as those who devote their full attention to options.

If you are already investing in other areas, such as day trading stocks, and are looking to branch out into options, then options trading can be a great complement to your current activities. Also, it's worth noting that your expectations make all the difference. If you have lofty ambitions, it might take you longer to hit your targets. So, do keep this in mind, too.

In this chapter, we are going to explore how you can make a regular income from trading options regardless of the specific amount of money you make. The point here is to set yourself up so that you can make a regular income regardless of the specific amount.

Starting Capital Required

A very common question asked by novice options traders is, "how much money do I need to get started?"

The answer to that question depends on your aims. If you are aiming to become a full-time options trader, you're going to need a larger starting capital. In contrast, if you're just looking to dip your toes into options trading, or are branching out from other investment activities, then you would need a smaller amount.

Here's a good rule of thumb to keep in mind.

- $5,000 is a good amount to start if you're looking to supplement your income, incorporate options into other activities such as day trading, or looking to begin your investing career. However, this is not a realistic amount if you are looking to become a full-time trader.

- $10,000 is a good amount for those looking to devote at least a part-time interest in options trading. For instance, swing traders that dabble in options generally start out with this amount. However, it may not be enough to become a full-time trader, at least not in the short term.

- $25,000 is the best amount for those looking to become full-time traders. You don't need to have the full amount on hand when you begin trading, but at least having the ability to eventually get it will help you set your sights on becoming a full-time trader.

- Please keep in mind that you don't need a large amount of money to get started with options. Nevertheless, if your aim is to make a living from investing in options, the more investment capital you have, the greater possibility of returns you have.

Income Generated from Options Trading

Another very common question is, "how much do options traders earn?"

This is a reasonable question to ask. After all, why would you invest in options if you won't make money? The idea here is to compensate for your time and effort appropriately. The main thing to keep in mind is that the amount you earn is largely dependent on the time and effort you invest in developing your trading skills.

So, let's take a look at how much you can reasonably expect to earn from options trading.

Full-time options traders can earn upwards of $100,000 a year. If you start out with $25,000 in investment capital and devote your full attention to options trading, it's certainly feasible to hit this target. However, it requires a great deal of effort and dedication to achieve this income level. It's not unheard of, but it's not quite so common. For average investors, reaching this plateau may seem unattainable.

Part-time traders, that are traders and investors who spend about 20 hours a week, can reasonably expect to earn about $1,000 a month or roughly $10,000 to $15,000 a year. However, it's important to note that not all trades are created equal. Therefore, some trades may provide you with higher profits while others not so much. If you're looking to supplement your monthly income, this would be a good target to aim for.

If you only occasionally dabble in options trading, it's reasonable to expect a few hundred dollars a month, or a few thousand per year. If you are not planning on dedicating much time to options trading, this could be a good starting point. Plenty of folks make modest profits early on as they learn the ropes. Eventually, they increase the amount of time they spend trading.

On the whole, the profit you make per trade may vary significantly. In some cases, you might make $1,000 or more on a single trade. In other cases, you might only make $50. Ultimately, it doesn't matter how much you make as long as you are making a profit. The worst thing that can happen is losing money on trades. So, making a profit, even a small one, is much better than taking a loss.

Frequency of Trading

One of the big reasons why full-time traders make so much money is because they place a high number of trades. For example, they place tens of trades a day. Naturally, they stand to make a good deal of money based on the sheer volume of trades they place. However, there is something important to consider here. You need to decide if your focus is going to be on short-term or long-term trades.

Short-term trades can last about one or two days. The reason for this is that you are looking to maximize the number of times you can make your money work for you. In some cases, you can take a small amount of capital and invest it many times over. In this case, you can generate small, but repeated profits. Ultimately, the small profits add up.

In contrast, if you only place a few trades per week, then the overall amount of profits would be less. Some experienced investors know how to make huge trades, that is, investments with large investment capital and significant margin. In such cases, you can make just as much, or even more, than frequent traders. In the end, it's about choosing an approach and going with it. Most importantly, making a conscious choice is pivotal in building your trading strategy.

Some investors like a combination of both. This approach implies a combination of frequent trades and long-term ones. Long-term trades can mean several days to several weeks. Many times, savvy investors can anticipate significant market shifts. However, they get in on the action early. That way, they can beat the market. Doing so implies tying up investments for a longer time frame. That is the reason why some investors don't like long-term trades. Nevertheless, long-term trades are the kind that can leave you with significant profits. So, it's worth keeping this approach in mind.

Rolling Over Profits

A good strategy some investors like to use is to roll over their earnings. In this strategy, investors take the proceeds they make from their first traders and add them up to their investment capital. That way, their investment capital grows and grows. What this enables investors to do is make larger traders. Therefore, the possibility of making a larger profit also increases.

Rolling over profits is quite useful, particularly when you don't actually need the money. This approach works when you're not desperate to make money. Instead, you can afford the luxury of letting your investments grow over time. Eventually, you can work your way up to a large investment capital that can enable you to make a decent income from options trading.

If you are looking to get into options trading in addition to swing or day trading, then rolling over your profits can help you cast a wider net across all of your trading activities. By implementing this strategy, you are looking more toward the future. But if you are looking for immediate returns, then rolling over your investments may not be the right approach for you. Nevertheless, you can always save a chunk of your earnings so you can reinvest them into your trading endeavors.

Trading in a Band

Trading in a band refers to buying and selling stocks when they are in a predictable range. When a stock trades in a band, its valuation fluctuates within "resistance" levels. There are two types of resistance levels. The first is the low end, that is, the "floor." The floor means that this is the lowest point a price will fall to before recovering. The second is the upper end known as the "ceiling." The ceiling refers to the highest point of a stock's price before falling back down.

When stocks trade in a range, investors can reasonably expect to determine the lowest and highest price points. As a result, this is the ultimate way of buying low and selling high. Since the price movements are rather predictable, it won't be hard for you to use options to help you make successful trades.

Here's how this strategy works.

To buy a stock at its lowest price point, you can use a call option with a strike price at the lowest price point you anticipate. To determine the floor, you can look at the historical data for the stock. Then, you can set up your call option at or slightly above the floor. In doing so, you can ensure that you can entice shareholders to sell. To maximize your profits, you can search for contracts that are close to expiration around the time you anticipate the price to fall. That way, you can purchase them at a discounted rate. Alternatively, you can purchase contracts with a longer expiration in case you feel you need more time.

The second part of the deal is to acquire a put option. The put option serves as the take-profit point of the trade. You can determine the ceiling by looking at the highest price points of the stock. Then, set up your put option slightly below the highest price point. That would entice your counterparty to pick up the stock as they would still have room to make another deal. Also, the put option serves as a means of protecting you in case price shifts happen sooner than expected. You could always buy a contract that's close to expiration. That way, you can minimize the impact of the premium on your deal.

The best way to make this trade work smoothly is to first exercise the call option, hold the stock, and then exercise the put option when it's close to the ceiling. That way, you don't run the risk of getting hit with an uncovered position. While selling before buying is quite common, it's also risky.

This band trading strategy is great for novice traders. It's also important to make sure you know how fast the price fluctuations will move. Many times, these fluctuations can happen in a matter of hours. So, you need to be ready to move quickly. Still, the use of automated trading can help you ease the process. Modern trading platforms allow you to automate your trades. When you automate your options, you don't need to be physically present to make the deal happen. The trading software simply executes the trades based on the parameters you have provided. For example, trades are executed when the strike price is reached. When this occurs, the software automatically exercises the option, no questions asked. Of course, it's always a good idea for you to be on top of your moves. Nevertheless, you can automate everything to help you move quickly without hesitation.

Chapter 8

Profiting from Covered Calls

In this strategy, the investor or trader goes about writing call options. However, there is an important aspect of writing a covered call. The investor or trader needs to hold a long position in the stock they are selling the call for. In other words, the writer actually owns the shares in question. That way, the investor can make good on their promise to furnish the stock should the option be exercised.

The reason why this strategy is called a "covered" call is that you have your position covered. In financial terminology, a covered position refers to any time you pledge something, money, or a stock, and you have what you need to complete the transaction. You can enter an options trade in a "naked" position when you agree to buy a stock but don't have the cash on hand to do it. Therefore, you need to get the money you to cover your position should the option be exercised.

In this situation, you need to produce the stock when the contract gets exercised. Failure to do so may lead you to get your account suspended (or terminated), you may get charges filed against you, or you may be hit with harsh penalties in addition to compensating the other party. Thus, it's not a good idea to make a mistake here.

When executed properly, covered calls can be a good way of making money on a regular basis. Most importantly, it's a safe way of ensuring that you profit from options trading. So, let's take a look at how you can make the most from a covered call.

Holding a Long Position

The term "long position" means that you own the stock specified in the agreement. Therefore, you don't have to worry about searching for shares in the event the option is exercised. As such, you own the shares outright. This means you can confidently pledge the shares in the trade.

It is important to note that you must hold a long position to make this trade. Some investors believe it's enough to hold another call option to make this trade work. However, you must be careful as simply having a contract may not be enough to make a profit. Nevertheless, holding an option for the stock itself could help you make the deal work in the event you don't actually have the shares on hand.

It's also worth noting that if you don't have the shares on hand at the time you write the contract, it's a good idea to get the shares as soon as possible. Otherwise, you may find yourself in trouble if the contract gets exercised immediately. So, not covering your position can lead to a series of difficulties down the road.

How a Covered Call Works

A covered call can work in one of two ways. In essence, you sell stock that you currently hold at a higher price than you paid for it. The way you got the shares in the first place doesn't really matter. Most of the time, options traders get hold of shares as a result of a put option they wrote.

Let's take a brief look at this point.

Let's assume that you wrote a put option. You pledged to purchase the stock of a corporation. So, you wrote the contract and collect the premium. Now, let's assume that your counterparty agreed to exercise the agreement.

So, you paid for the shares at the agreed price point. You now own shares of the company in question.

At this point, you could do one of two things. If the current valuation is higher than your purchase price, you could simply sell them straight up. That would be the quickest way to make your money back, and then some.

The second thing that you could do is hold on to the shares. This makes sense when the current market valuation is lower than the price you paid for them. For instance, if you paid $6 per share, but the current market valuation is $5.50, then it makes sense for the price to rise. That way, you stand to profit when the buyer exercises the option.

Now, you might be thinking, "why would an investor agree to an option at a price point higher than its current market valuation?"

That is a valid question.

You see, most investors learn to anticipate moves. If investors feel that the current market valuation is temporary, they may be inclined to purchase a call option in case of the share price spikes. So, you can issue a call option with a strike price of $6.25. At this price point, it makes sense for investors to protect themselves.

Another important reason why investors would choose the options contract is that they lack sufficient funds at that point. So, they can't buy the shares even though they want to. Therefore, getting an option makes the most sense.

Lastly, investors choose to purchase options just in case. There are times when investors are not keen to act immediately. Instead, they opt for a "wait and see attitude." This attitude is common when investors are waiting for factors to play out.

So, you now own shares in this corporation and are prepared to write a call option. When you do so, you collect the premium on the contract and agree to furnish the shares if and when the investor chooses to go through with it.

Now, let's suppose you have found a taker for the contract. The agreement is to sell 100 shares of the corporation at $6.25. Please bear in mind that you paid $6 apiece. As such, this valuation lands you a $0.25 profit. Additionally, you collected a premium of $10. If the contract goes unused, you keep the shares plus the $10 premium.

Let's now assume that the contract is used. So, you know receive payment for the shares, plus the premium. In exchange, you deliver the 100 shares of the corporation in question. This concludes the transactions.

Here is the breakdown of how the transaction played out:

- Income received from the premium $10
- Income received from the total sale of stock $625
- The total amount paid for the stock $600
- Gross profit $35

In this example, the investor profited $35 from the transaction. The proceeds came from the sale of the contract (premium) and the stock. When discounting the amount paid for the stock originally, the gross profits are calculated. Now, it's important to note that we say it "gross" as there may be taxes levied on profits. Taxes vary from state to state. So, it's worth checking out what your state's laws are on taxing income derived from stock market transactions.

Also, this example highlights how covered calls are very safe transactions. This means that you don't have a high degree of risk in this transaction as you are selling something that you own. As such, there are no complications to be concerned about. All you need to make sure is that the contract gets exercised. Otherwise, you pocket the premium without surrendering the shares.

Things to Avoid in a Covered Call

When going into a covered call, there are a few things to consider. So, let's take a look at what you should avoid when conducting a covered call.

Don't pledge more stock than you own

One of the temptations that you must resist is to pledge more shares than you own. For example, if you own 100 shares of a given stock, you must avoid writing two or three contracts using the same stock. The problem lies with multiple contracts being exercised at the same time. So, if you owned 100 shares, but pledge 300, you would have an uncovered position of 200 shares.

In this type of scenario, you could make up the difference by owning additional options to cover your open position. However, if you don't have some type of backup position, you might end up getting into trouble. The worst thing that you could do is hope that contracts don't get exercised. Naturally, this is a situation that would not place you in a favorable position. So, always make sure you have enough shares to cover any open contracts.

Don't be afraid to buy it back

In cases where the share price skyrockets, you might find that the contract holder has a much lower price compared to the current market value. So, if you let the contract holder keep the agreement, they might exercise the option leaving you with less than you could have earned. So, don't be afraid to buy back the option. Even if you break even, that is, pay back the premium, you still stand to make more money by selling at current market prices.

Now, this strategy works right before the price takes off. If you choose to buy it back after the price jumps, the contract holder may not want to sell. So, this is where you need to anticipate future price movements. If you believe the price will take off, then you might want to be proactive and buy the contract back right in time. Then, you can sell the stock at much higher market valuation.

Don't wait too long

One of the biggest issues with covered calls is expiration. If you let your shares sit by idly for too long, you might end up losing more money in the long run. The reasoning here is that idle shares mean money that you can't invest elsewhere. As such, selling off your shares, and taking those proceeds for other investments makes a significant difference.

If you find the contract running a bit long, you can buy it back and sell off your shares elsewhere, or you can sell the stock and buy an option. The important thing here is to avoid leaving your position uncovered. If you're confident that the option will go unused, you might consider selling off your shares close to the end of expiration. However, it's best to buy the option back close to expiration. You could still keep a portion of the premium.

Don't make covered calls with highly liquid stocks

When you have highly liquid stock, that is stocks you can sell quickly, don't take out a covered call. In this case, it's best to simply hold on to them and sell when you need to. There won't be any shortage of buyers. So, simply making a straight sale is the best way to avoid having your money tied up for too long.

It's also important to consider that highly liquid stocks don't lose much value over time. So, you can either choose to keep the stock for yourself or sit on it and sell when you really need it. In any event, it might make sense to issue a covered call in a very short-term contract. That way, you won't be subject to the contract's expiration. Instead, you can wait out the contract if necessary, but its expiration won't be exceedingly long.

On the whole, covered calls are a great way for you to make consistent money every time you take ownership of a stock. Just make sure that you don't dabble in illiquid stocks. Otherwise, it might be hard for you to find takers. Still, covered calls are one of the go-to alternatives for options traders. They are quite simple to set up and safe to deal with. After all, there is no risk of default if you own the shares. As long as you follow the recommended guidelines, you'll be in great shape.

Chapter 9

Profiting from Naked Puts

A naked put is essentially the opposite of a covered call. The term "naked" refers to the fact that the option writer does not own the stock pledged in the agreement. Therefore, the writer issues a contract in which they agree to buy the stock in question without having sufficient funds to cover their position. As such, if the option were to be exercised, the writer would be on the hook for the purchase of the shares. This would pose a problem for the writer if they were unable to produce the required funds for the purchase.

In short, a naked put is a put option in which the contract's writer doesn't have any intention of fulfilling. This is a risky strategy but profitable if the contract does not get exercised. The intention behind a naked put is to generate income through the premium on the contract. This strategy works very well at producing regular income based on premiums. However, great care needs to be taken that the stock does not rise significantly in price.

In this chapter, we are going to take a look at how a naked put works, and how you can use it to make profits. However, please be warned that this is a risky transaction. So, it's important for you to be careful. Otherwise, you might get stuck with a margin call. At that point, you would need to come up with the funds to purchase the stock. Needless to say, you don't want to liquidate valuable stocks just to cover a bad move.

How a Naked Put Works

When traders write put options, they agree to buy the stock in question should the contract get exercised. So, the writer does not own the stock. The contract holder owns the stock. If the contract holder chooses to exercise the contract, then the writer needs to pay for the stock. Therefore, the writer needs to be sure they have the fund or at least the means to get them, in order to cover their open position. In this case, the writer enters the put option in a short position. The term "short" means that they do not have the necessary funds to cover their open position.

Now, the writer can pull this off if the stock in question does not fall below the strike price on the contract. As long as the market price is higher, the contract holder would have no need to exercise the contract. However, if the price falls below the agreed price on the deal, then the contract holder may be compelled to exercise their right. After all, the price of the contract is higher than its current market valuation.

Please bear in mind that a put option favors the rightsholder only when the price on the agreement is higher than the current market valuation. As long as the market valuation is higher, the contract doesn't provide enough value. As such, the rightsholder may choose to keep the agreement just in case. However, they won't feel compelled to use it unless the market changes. Therefore, to make naked put work really well, you need to be reasonably sure that the fluctuations in the market won't lead the stock to fall below the strike price specified in the agreement.

Let's take a look at an example of this situation:

An options trader writes a put for a company's stock. The agreement is for 100 shares at $8 apiece. The writer agrees to purchase the 100 shares if the rightsholder chooses to exercise the option. Additionally, the contract has a $15 premium. So, the writer collects the

$15 premium while standing by. The stock's current share price stands at $8.50. This price point means that it is better to sell the stock straight up than to exercise the contract. As long as this price point holds, the writer needs not to worry about the contract by using. However, if the price falls below $8, then the writer may have cause for concern.

At this point, you might be thinking, "why would the rightsholder purchase a put option that's got a lower strike price than current market valuations?"

The answer to that is relatively straightforward.

For the rightsholder, this contract represents a safe haven. It is a hedge in case the market valuation for their stock falls below a specific threshold. As such, it works as a stop-loss for the seller. That's why naked puts are a good deal as they provide cover for shareholders who simply want an exit strategy should the deal not work out in their favor. This is the reason why the contract writer needs to be reasonably sure that the price will hold. Otherwise, the writer may get stuck with having to purchase stock they don't want to buy.

In the event that the writer does have to purchase the stock, the investor now has shares they can use for a covered call. This is generally the way these deals work. If the investor is forced to buy the stock, they can do so at a discounted rate. Therefore, the stock works favorably for a covered call afterward.

Let's break down the transaction:

- The premium on the contract: $15
- Total share price paid: $800 (100 shares at $8 apiece)
- The total amount paid: $785

Now, here is where it works out in the writer's favor. Even though the writer paid $8 per share in the deal, they kept the $15 premium. So, that offsets the price of the shares themselves. Therefore, the writer really paid $7.65 per share ($765 / 100 = $7.65). As such, the writer still got a deal on the shares. Ultimately, the writer can then turnaround and make a covered call for a much larger profit. So, the writer doesn't lose out on the deal.

It's worth noting that the only way the writer would lose money on the deal is if the shares plummet. For instance, let's assume the shares plummet to $5 apiece.

In that case, the writer would be hard-pressed to make any money on this deal. Nevertheless, if the shares remain anywhere above $7.65 per share, the investor stands to make money.

In cases where the contract is exercised, writers don't make a profit on the put option. They can make that up on the covered call. Also, if the stock's price spikes significantly, then the writer can sell the stock straight up on current market prices. In a way, a naked put serves as a means of making a larger deal down the road.

Things to Look Out for in a Naked Put

When you're dealing with a naked put, there are a few things to consider.

Don't commit to contracts over 100 shares apiece

Committing to contracts over 100 shares apiece is a big mistake. The reason for this is that positions greater than 100 shares open the door for greater risk. Therefore, it's important to ensure that you don't elevate your risk needlessly. If you are keen on making deals for a larger number of shares, it's best to issue individual contracts of 100 shares apiece.

The most important advantage that comes with dealing in 100-share lots is that you can always buy individual contracts back. That gives you the flexibility to buy the back one by one as needed. However, if you sell one, large contract, it might be very difficult for you to buy it back later on. As such, you would need to come up with the cash to cover the premium on the buyback. Likewise, if the contract is exercised, your naked position may end up putting you in a tight spot. Generally, this implies having to liquidate other valuable assets just to cover the naked position. So, writing individual contracts is always the best way to do.

Always have an exit strategy

The worst thing you can do when you write a put option is to assume that the contract holder will not exercise it. In fact, you should always assume that the contract will be exercised. So, this means that you should have an exit strategy in case you are forced to purchase the stock.

One way to protect yourself is to have highly liquid assets you can sell. For example, high-quality stocks are always easy to sell. Also, you may have put options of your own. While you are no looking to sell the stocks, you have the agreements in place should you need to use them. Other investors like to have a cash slice they can dip into in case they have any urgent needs.

Please bear in mind that when you have a naked position, you don't currently have the cash on hand to cover the position. However, you should have a reasonable plan to get the funds should you need them. Investors run into serious trouble when they cannot cover naked positions. Improvisation usually leads to mistakes and losses. So, always having an exit strategy for a naked put is a must.

Always study the market

When going about naked puts, always study the market. Please bear in mind that your biggest enemy is falling stock prices. As such, you need to make sure that the stock in question does not fall below the strike price on the agreement. Therefore, using a put option as a stop-loss makes sense for the contract holder. In doing so, they take out some insurance in case things don't work out for them. As for you, as the contract writer, you collect with the premium without having to dish out the funds for the stock itself.

Please be aware of market fluctuations. If the market shows wild swings, then it might be best to refrain from going about a naked put. While you can certainly sell puts, amid wild market swings, make sure you have your position covered. That way, you are ready in case the option is used. It will save you a great deal of problems down the road.

If you are unfamiliar with a specific stock or industry, it would be best to avoid entering a naked position. That's why it's always recommended that you do your best to make sure you have a good understanding of where the market is headed.

Beware of short-term naked puts

Short-term but generally tend to be exercised more often than long-term ones. The reason for this is because the contract holder is anticipating movements in a brief timeframe. Thus, this puts you on the spot. If you plan to sell a naked put, you are opening the door for trouble. So, if you do write a short-term put, please make sure that you have your position covered.

One of the best ways to avoid this is if you are holding other puts. In this case, you hold a contract for other stock which you can turn around and sell if you need money in a pinch. That way, you won't be affected should the put you wrote get called in.

Write naked puts for stocks you are willing to buy

Writing puts, in general, can be a challenge as you may find yourself buying shares you don't want. As such, it's always a good idea to write puts for stocks that you are willing to buy for yourself. These stocks can be shares that you would like to hold on to as part of a buy and hold strategy or stock that you know you can quickly turn around and sell. Ideally, the stocks in question would be highly liquid stocks that are in high demand. Please refrain from writing puts for stocks that don't have much traction. Doing so may put you in a spot where you might have a hard time dumping the stock, especially in a short timeframe. So, it's always a good idea to focus on stocks you have an interest in owning. That way, you can be certain that if you do have to purchase them, you won't be stuck with an asset that's not of your interest.

Chapter 10

How to Short a Stock Using Options

Shorting stocks is a mythical process that most traders dream about. The reason why shorting stocks is considered to be so profitable is that the potential for making significant deals is extremely high. Often, traders short stocks that most investors would not imagine. Yet, when these deals work out, they can prove to be a true home run.

If you are interested in getting a pretty detailed account of how shorting works, check out the Hollywood film, "The Big Short." In this film, you will find a fictional account of traders who hit one to the moon. It is based on actual events surrounding the 2008 financial crisis. Its definition worth spending some time on it.

For the practical purpose of this book, we will look at how shorting stocks works in real life. We will be looking at straightforward examples that you can apply in your everyday trading life. As such, we won't be discussing multimillion-dollar deals. We will be focusing on deals that you can turn into your bread-and-butter tactics.

It's also important to remember that shorting stocks is highly risky. So, it's essential that you carefully study what you plan to do. Otherwise, you may open the door for trouble. If you're not careful, you could find yourself in a tight squeeze. In some cases, you might have to liquidate other assets. In the worst of cases, you may have to go into debt to cover your margins. Therefore, it is of the utmost importance that you take care of your trades.

Overview of Shorting Stocks

A short position is when you enter a trade or agreement in which you do not own the asset or have the fund to cover the open position. Consequently, a "short" position is the exact opposite of a "long" position. In a long position, you have ownership of the asset or you have the funds to cover an open position. In a short position, you are completely exposed. This means that if the deal is called in, you stand to take a serious hit.

Here is a good example of how a short position works.

You go to the track to place a bet on a horse race. You pick the horse of your choice and place the bet. Let's assume that you bet $100 on a specific horse. Now, if you win, you collect your deposit plus your winnings. If you lose, you need to cover the bet. The bookie who took your bet does not ask for any money upfront. They may ask you for a smaller deposit to secure the deal.

If you win, the bookie will call you to ask you if you'd like to collect or rollover your bet. If you lose, the bookie will call to collect. Let's assume that you lost. So, the bookie is now calling to collect the $100. At this point, you have no choice but to pay. However, there would be a problem if you didn't have the money. In that case, you would have a set amount of time to come up with it. If you fail to pay, the bookie may resort to other means of collection.

As you can see, shorting a stock is like placing a bet. If the bet works out, you win. If the bet doesn't work out, then you may need to figure out a way to cover your end of the agreement. Therefore, traders who short stocks must be aware of the possible fluctuations in the market. This is the reason why doing your homework is essential when it comes to successfully shorting stocks.

Example of a Short Sale

Let's take a look at a sample short sale.

A corporation's stock currently sits at $11 a share. This corporation has a high trade volume. In other words, it is a popular stock. So, there is no shortage of buyers of sellers for this corporation's shares. Since you are keen on making a good return but don't have much money to invest, you figure a short sale would work. So, you look into purchasing a put option for this corporation's stock.

According to expert estimates and your research, this corporation's share price is expected to climb in the near future. Past highs for the stock place the share price around $14 a share. Consequently, it is reasonable to assume that its stock price will reach $14. To play it safe, you assume that $13 per share is a fair target to aim for.

At this point, you have two options. You can either search for an existing put option for this corporation with a strike price hovering around the $13-mark or purchase a brand-new agreement. Let's assume that you found an existing agreement with about a week left on its expiration. Thus, you manage to purchase it for a fraction of the original premium. Upon issue, its premium is valued at $100. You managed to snag it for $25. You now own a put option to sell 100 shares of this corporation at $13 apiece.

Now, here is the tricky part, you have a put option to sell a stock that you don't yet own. This leaves you with two alternatives. The first alternative is to purchase the shares upfront. If you do so, then you would no longer have a short position as you own the shares. This would be a smart move if you have the money and the shares at a good price. The second alternative is to purchase a call option for a profitable price point. Since your current put option is valued at $13 apiece, you would need a call option below the $13 threshold. Now, let's assume you found an open contract with about a week left on it. The price indicated on this contract is for $11.50 a share. Automatically, you have a call option for the stock at a reasonable price. Additionally, the premium on it was down from $100 to $25 given the term left on the agreement.

The easy part here would be to exercise the put option first, collect the money, and then exercise the call option. With the proceeds from the put option, you can pay for the shares in the call. In this example, you have successfully pulled off a short sale.

Let's review the main points:

- This deal was successful because you owned a put and call. So, all you needed to do was exercise the agreements. The counterparty in the put option didn't have much choice. Once you executed the put, they were obligated to pay for the stock. You were able to make money as the call option was valued at a favorable price point compared to the put.

- The put was valued at a higher price point than the call.

- You had offsetting positions. This ensures that you won't risk defaulting on the deal.

Let's look at the profits.

- Call option: 100 shares at $11.50 = $1,150 + $25 premium, total paid = $1,175.

- Put option: 100 shares at $13 = $1,300 - $25 premium, total paid = $1,275

- Total profit: $1,275 - $1,175 = $100.

In this example, you earned $100 from a $50 investment. In essence, you doubled the money you invested in the premium paid in the purchase of the shares. As a result, you doubled your money by trading a total of $2,450 worth of stocks with only $50 down.

Now, let's take a look at another, more complex example.

You write a call option for the same corporation in question. Its share price sits at $11. You write the call option for $11.50 apiece. This means that if the contract holder chooses to exercise the option, you would be on the hook for 100 of this corporation's stock at $11.50. You collect $100 for the premium on the contract.

On the surface, this call option doesn't seem like it will be used as the strike price is higher than the current market price. The contract holder agrees to purchase the call as they anticipate the price will bust through to the $14 mark. In that case, $11.50 would make sense to them.

All of a sudden, you are in a short position as you do not own the shares you need. Unliked a naked put, you are in a "naked call." The difference is that in the naked put you need to pay for the shares. In the naked call, you need to furnish the shares.

To cover your position, you need to buy shares that are valued below the $11.50 mark. In this case, you purchase a call option at $11.00, or right at the current market value. This agreement makes sense as the writer of the option anticipates the price of the stock to remain at the $11 mark. In this agreement, you hold the right to buy the shares if need be. Since this option is currently "at the money," meaning that it's the same price as the current market valuation, you get a discount on the premium. So, you pay $50 for the whole contract.

Here is one very important thing to keep in mind. The contract that you purchase must have a longer expiration than the one you sold. The reason for this is based on the expectation that the contract you wrote will be exercised first. Therefore, you need more time to eventually cover your short position.

If the share price stays at $11, none of the contracts stand to be exercised. So, let's assume that the price shoots up past $12 and lands at $13. The rightsholder of the call you wrote exercises the option at $11.50. They pay you $1,150 for the 100 shares. You are now on the clock. You need to furnish the shares within the timeframe specified in the option you wrote. So, you turn around and exercise your call at $11 apiece. You pay $1,100 for the shares. Then, you deliver the shares to the counterparty on the call you wrote. At this point, the deal is finalized.

Let's examine this deal in closer detail.

- You wrote one call and purchased another.
- You didn't invest any money upfront. You collected the $100 premium from the first option and then paid $50 for the other call.
- You were paid for the shares first and then used those proceeds to pay for the shares you delivered to your counterparty.

Here's the profit breakdown.

- You wrote a call for $100. You received $1,150. So, $1,150 + $100 = $1,250.00
- You purchased a call for $50. You paid $1,100 for the stock. So, $1,100 + $50 = $1,150.00
- You profited $100 from this deal ($1,250 - $1,150)

While the profit is the same, you made an infinite return on your investment. The reason why it's "infinite" is that you didn't invest anything in the deal. All you did was write one option and purchase another contract with the premium you received from the option you wrote. In contrast, the first example required you to invest some money upfront. It's also worth noting that you made the same profit in monetary terms in a much tighter range. Hence, this deal was much more feasible than the first.

As you can see, it is quite possible to make money trading options without putting up anything upfront. However, shorting stocks can be quite risky. In both examples, we assumed the price shot up. Had the price gone down, the contracts would not have been exercised. Therefore, you would have lost money on the deal as the premiums you paid would not have produced any income. In the first scenario, you would have lost $100. In the second one, you would have made a $50 profit on the premiums. This is the reason why shorting stocks can be quite risky. Nevertheless, doing your research can help you make the most of your investments. So, do make sure you always do your homework. The time you put in before going into a deal will save you money and headaches down the road.

Conclusion

Well, there it is! We have covered everything you need to know about trading options. Now, you are ready to get started in the world of financial markets. If you already have experience trading, then you are certainly ready to make the most of your trading endeavors. If you are brand new, then you will find this guide provided you with the right setup.

So, this is the time to get started. This is the time to make the most of your time and effort. While we have outlined how important it is to have enough start-up capital, we have also highlighted how you can make trades with very little money. Therefore, the world is at your fingertips. All you need is to make the choice to get started today.

The next step is to take everything you have learned and put it to the test. Often, this means failing at the first few trades you make. But you will also get it right, too. That's why this guide is the type of book you need to walk you through your first few trades. As you gain more and more experience, you will find that mastering options are a question of time and experience. The more practice you have, the easier it will be for you to make some serious money. While you may not make a full-time living from options, you'll find that the tools are there. If you ever needed to make a full-time living from options, you have the toolkit to get you there.

Thank you very much for taking the time to read this book. We are sure that you got a lot out of it. If you enjoyed it and found it useful, please tell your friends, family, and colleagues about it. Please tell anyone that you feel would be interested in learning more about options trading. They too will benefit from this book just like you have.

Please remember that you have everything you need to be successful. There is no time to waste. There are plenty of other people, just like you, who started from the beginning and worked their way to the top. You don't need any special skill set to master options. Often, the right knowledge and some elbow grease are enough to get things off the ground.

So, what are you waiting for?

Let's get started making some serious money with options. You'll be so glad you tried your best. Your future self is already thanking you for the decisions you made today.

Good luck and happy investing!

Description

Are you seeking a new and safe way of investing your money without exposing yourself to risk?

Are you seeking for a way to invest your hard-earned cash without falling into marketing gimmicks?

Are you seeking a tried and true way of making money that isn't filled with the promises of get-rich-quick schemes?

Are you seeking a road to financial freedom so that you won't have to depend on a job anymore?

If you answered "yes" to any of these questions, then this is the book for you. In this volume, we will be talking about the world of options trading. If you are looking to make some serious money in the stock market, options are the way for you to go. You don't need any fancy college degrees. All you need is the information in this book and some good, old-fashioned elbow grease. The rest is up to you.

In this book, you will find the tools that you need to make the most of options. You will learn about trading stocks by using contracts. These contracts are agreements that will help you steer clear of trouble while capitalizing on market trends.

Here is a glimpse of what you can learn in this book.

The fundamentals of options trading and the right strategies used to make money.

The ins and outs of call and put options and how you can cash in on any type of market situation.

How to make money during a bear market, especially when other investors are losing money.

How to cash in on a bull market, especially when optimism is riding high among investors.

Using leverage to magnify your trades while using very little investment capital to make them work.

Simple, yet effective, examples of how options trades are conducted in real life.

Clear guidelines that you can follow so that you are able to develop a clear trading strategy.

Easy to follow instructions on trades that you can implement right away.

How to make the most of market fluctuations and the use of options to protect your investments.

The right way to manage risk, particularly when market conditions are not optimal.

This book is chock full of industry secrets the experts don't want you to know. But we have laid them out for you. So, you don't need to pay hefty commissions to stockbrokers and fund managers. You have all the tools you need to take control of your investments. Plus, you don't need to pay thousands and thousands of dollars in courses, seminars, and consulting fees. Everything you need to get started is right here.

So, what are you waiting for?

Take the time to get started on what could be the most profitable journey of your life. If you fail to act now, there is no telling how hard it might be for you to attain financial freedom. After all, we all seek the comfort and peace of mind that comes with knowing you have your finances sorted out.

There is no time like today to get started. So, let's get on the road that leads to financial freedom today!

www.ingramcontent.com/pod-product-compliance
Lightning Source LLC
Chambersburg PA
CBHW070653220526
45466CB00001B/414